DIG DIG DI
FOR FOR FO
VICTORY VICTORY VICTO

DIG DIG DIG
FOR FOR FOR
TORY VICTORY VICTORY

DIG DIG DI
FOR FOR FO
VICTORY VICTORY VICTO

DIG DIG DIG
FOR FOR FOR
TORY VICTORY VICTORY

DIG DIG DI
FOR FOR FO
VICTORY VICTORY VICTO

DIG
FOR
VICTORY

DIG FOR VICTORY

Summersdale Publishers Ltd
46 West Street
Chichester
West Sussex
PO19 1RP
UK

www.summersdale.com

Printed and bound in China

ISBN: 978-1-84953-276-1

Substantial discounts on bulk quantities of Summersdale books are available to corporations, professional associations and other organisations. For details telephone Summersdale Publishers on (+44-1243-771107), fax (+44-1243-786300) or email (nicky@summersdale.com).

DIG
FOR
VICTORY

CONTENTS

INTRODUCTION

The original 'Dig for Victory' campaign during the war years encouraged families to work their gardens and take on allotments in order to supplement rationing. As we are once again faced with times of austerity, people are rediscovering the value of their gardens and hedgerows and realising that not only do home-grown fruits and vegetables taste better, but you know that your produce is chemical-free and so much cheaper (and more rewarding) than buying it from the supermarket. The physical benefits of gardening are also not to be sniffed at. Working in the garden can be as strenuous as any gym workout, with the added benefit of being outside, breathing in fresh air.

Tending a garden and reaping the benefits can leave you glowing with pride (and health), and this little book of invaluable tips, interspersed with sage quotes from the green-fingered to cheer you on, is all you need to make your garden grow and get digging for victory.

GARDEN TOOLS AND EQUIPMENT

Cut up old stockings and tights into strips to make plant ties – the soft, flexible nature of the fabric will protect new shoots as they grow bigger.

Ties from packaged loaves are also good for securing climbing plants to stakes.

An old potato peeler makes an excellent job of removing weeds from the lawn.

Make sure to invest in a water butt that is connected to a down pipe from a gutter. Rain water can be preserved in this way and it beats using a hosepipe to water plants in the summer.

Repair a leaky hosepipe by plugging any puncture holes with toothpicks, saving water and money.

Alternatively, if your hose is beyond repair, make a few more holes in it and use it as a sprinkler for the vegetable patch or lawn.

Take thy plastic spade,
It is thy pencil; take thy
seeds, thy plants,
They are thy colours.

William Mason, *The English Garden*

To a gardener there is
nothing more exasperating
than a hose that just isn't
long enough.

Cecil Roberts, *Gone Rustic*

Good quality second-hand gardening equipment can be picked up very cheaply – and sometimes even for free. Before you buy anything new, look on the Freecycle website. You will find a dedicated Freecycle community in your area and all the items are free! Car boot sales and recycling centres are also great places to pick up gardening equipment at bargain prices.

If your garden gloves are looking a little tatty, give them a wash and turn them inside out.

Stones make great plant markers. Clean and dry them and label using a permanent marker.

Lolly sticks are also perfect for plant markers.

Make a garden kneeler by filling an old
hot-water bottle with polystyrene chips. It's
wipe-clean and will make those long hours in
the garden a little more comfortable.

An ice cream container can be cut up to
make multiple waterproof plant markers.

Curtain rods, particularly extendable ones, are perfect for training tall climbing plants. Simply extend the rod as the plant grows!

There's no need to invest in a dibber – a screwdriver will do the same job.

Don't spend money on supporting canes;
instead use twigs. They look far less
conspicuous and they're free!

Alternatively, grow your own bamboo canes
to support sweet peas and other climbing
plants. Bamboo can grow to 3 metres or
more and makes attractive screens. Harvest
the canes in the autumn and dry them flat in
a garage or shed.

Willow will also provide stakes and hurdles for plants.

Save all packaging from shop-bought food items – these trays and cartons can be used to plant seedlings. Supermarkets and greengrocers regularly throw out wooden and plastic crates which make great planters.

The little plastic cups at the water cooler are ideal for seed-starting plots.

Keep the inner tubes of toilet rolls and kitchen rolls to plant seedlings. The plants can go straight into the ground, still in the tube, as the cardboard will biodegrade.

The array of food packaging that tends to gather in the recycling bin can be used as both pots and cloches. Tin cans make lovely planters, especially on a kitchen windowsill.

When you've finished with plastic drinks bottles, make cloches to protect new plants by cutting the bottoms off. Place firmly in the ground to protect the plants from slugs and remove the bottle tops when the plants are more established to allow them to acclimatise.

Plastic bottles can also be used as irrigation devices. Pierce holes in the sides around the base and partially bury them in the flowerbeds. Fill them as needed, and your blooms will have a steady, gradual supply of water.

Use an old broom handle to make your seed trenches by laying the handle along the soil and pressing it down firmly, leaving a trench an inch deep.

Make your own fruit cage with wooden posts and plastic netting. These are often longer-lasting and a fraction of the price of the ready-made ones.

An old Parmesan cheese shaker is perfect for spreading seeds. Simply mix fine seeds with sand and sprinkle where required.

If you are starting off your seedlings in a greenhouse, you can reduce your heating costs by hanging plastic sheeting across the greenhouse and only heating the area that contains the seedlings. Use bubble wrap to insulate the door and block any draughts.

If you don't have a greenhouse, polytunnels are an inexpensive alternative and they are easy to manoeuvre round the garden.

Look after your tools. Here are a few tips:

- Keep tools rust-free and good as new by having an oily rag to hand in the garden shed and wiping them after use at the end of the day.

- Store tools away from ground level as garages and sheds can be quite damp. Hang tools up if you can.

• Use antibacterial wipes when cleaning pruners between cuts to keep plants healthy and disease-free.

• Treat your lawnmower to an annual service and it will keep going for many years to come.

FRUIT AND VEGETABLES

Gently bruise garlic cloves by squeezing
them between your thumb and forefinger
before planting them as this will make them
more flavoursome.

Hang mothballs on your peach trees to
prevent leaf curl.

Digging potatoes is always an adventure, somewhat akin to fishing. There is forever the possibility that the next cast – or the next thrust of the digging fork – will turn up a clunker.

Jerome Belanger

It's difficult to think
anything but pleasant
thoughts while eating a
home-grown tomato.

Lewis Grizzard

Treat your veg patch once you have harvested your autumn vegetables. Dig out any weeds and go over with a good dose of compost and manure, then cover with old rugs or an unwanted carpet for the winter – you'll have the perfect base to start spring planting the next year.

Use an old pair of tights to store onions. Tie a knot between each onion so that they are not touching, then hang up in a dry place, such as a pantry. When you need to take an onion, simply cut below the knot.

When planning what to plant in your vegetable patch, think about what your family eats regularly. So if you eat a lot of apples, carrots and potatoes, plant them rather than growing something more unusual which won't get eaten.

To maximise your plot, plant two vegetable crops in the same furrow by mixing a fast-growing vegetable, such as lettuce, with a slow-growing one, such as parsnip or carrot. Alternatively, you can keep sowing the same type of vegetable every few weeks, wait for the first crop to be at the thinning stage and sow again.

Using old spare tyres as planters for potatoes or carrots is eco-friendly and effective. For carrots, a sandy mix soil in a two-deep tyre container will give you lovely and straight crops, free of pests (carrot fly can only fly to around 2 ft so if the tyre wall is high enough they cannot attack young plants). For potatoes, plant chitted tubers one tyre deep, wait for plants to grow, bank up with soil and add more tyres to the stack (up to about three tyres deep). Once the plants have flowered the potatoes are ready to harvest.

Dustbins, compost bags and bark bags are also good for growing potatoes in. If using bags, keep unrolling them and adding more compost as the potatoes grow.

Old plastic guttering is great for irrigating the vegetable patch. Drill small holes along the half-tubes, lay it alongside your row of vegetables and pour water into one end for an even distribution.

Keep your cabbage crop far away from strawberries as they do not make good companions – the cabbage plants will kill off the strawberries.

Brambles may be a little unsightly in a tended garden, but consider keeping an area wild as this will attract beneficial creatures into the garden, such as slow-worms and frogs, and the brambles will reward you with blackberries in the summer.

Plant marigolds (or *Calendula*) near or in your vegetable patch to provide shelter for insects that will benefit your crop.

Lay straw around your strawberries to keep the fruits off the ground and protected from grey mould.

Sow different varieties of lettuce from late March to July in rows roughly 15 cm apart – lettuce can be grown close together to produce baby leaves for salads. Harvest the leaves as soon as they are a few inches long – the plants will regrow so that you can continue to 'cut and come again'.

Melons are prone to rot. Reduce this risk by
placing flat stone or concrete beneath
the fruit.

Alternatively, grow melons in the greenhouse
and use string bags or strong tights to
support the weighty fruits.

Increase the size of artichoke heads by making two incisions in the fully developed stalk just below the head and inserting two criss-crossing matchsticks.

If you don't have space to grow vegetables, or the amount that you would like to produce, consider taking on an allotment, or perhaps sharing a plot with one or two friends.

And he gave it for his opinion that
whoever could make two ears
of corn, or two blades of grass,
to grow upon a spot of ground
where only one grew before, would
deserve better of mankind, and
do more essential service to his
country, than the whole race of
politicians put together.

Jonathan Swift, *Gulliver's Travels*

In order to live off a garden,
you practically have to
live in it.

Kin Hubbard

Rather than buying expensive cloches to protect your potato seedlings, use sheets of old newspaper weighted down with stones – it may look unattractive but they can be removed in the morning.

Try storing apples the way that US growers do by placing them between layers of maple leaves. This practice can also be used for storing root vegetables.

If you are lucky enough to have a glut of fruit and vegetables from your harvest, there are a number of ways that it can be stored:

• All fruits can be dried, but only use blemish-free fruits for this. Wash, pit and slice the fruits, then blanch them by steaming for five minutes then plunging the pieces into cold water. Dip them in a mixture of water and lemon juice to reduce browning and leave them to dry on some kitchen towel. Once completely dry, place on parchment-lined baking trays and place them in the oven on a low heat for four hours. Let them stand overnight and then freeze them in sealed bags until required.

• Strawberries, raspberries, currants and hedgerow fruits can be frozen. Open-freeze the fruits by spreading them on trays and placing directly in the freezer. Once frozen, decant them into plastic bags and seal them.

• Pears and apples should be wrapped individually in newspaper and stored in wooden boxes or drawers in a cool, dark place. An unheated garage or shed is ideal. Check on the fruits regularly for ones that have gone off.

- If you have the shed or garage space, pick up an old chest of drawers from a junk shop and use it to store your vegetables. Spread a layer of sand at the bottom of each draw and place a layer of vegetables on top. Then cover the vegetables with sand and add more vegetables on top until you reach the top of the draw. Label and date the drawers.

- Potatoes can be scrubbed and stored in hessian sacks in a cool, dry place.

• Don't discard windfall fruit; it can be used to make delicious chutney, or frozen and later defrosted to provide a treat for birds in the depths of winter.

Keep the stalks attached to your cherries and strawberries when harvesting as it helps to maintain their freshness.

PLANTING AND TENDING

Collect fallen leaves when they are wet, then store in bin bags for two years. The result is a nutritious leaf mulch which can be used to cover your most prized plants.

Alternatively, make a bin out of chicken wire or mesh and store your leaves in there for mulching. Oak leaves are particularly good for compost as they reduce slug and snail infestations, and birch leaves have disinfectant properties which will prevent fly diseases.

To bring on seedlings, use either a seed tray, old newspapers, rolled and fashioned into napkin ring-shaped rounds, or toilet roll tubes cut in half. Fill with compost, add seeds according to planting instructions on the packet and water regularly. Once seedlings are ready to be planted out, take the round and transplant directly into the ground. The paper or cardboard will biodegrade and the root system of your seedling will not be destroyed.

Cardboard can.be added to compost heaps to make a good mulch. It also suppresses weeds.

The cheapest compost is the compost that you make yourself. All manner of things can be composted. Human hair in seed trenches will not only add useful trace elements but also entangle nasty bugs as they try to destroy your seedlings.

Use only organic waste for your compost – kitchen scraps, grass cuttings, etc. – and be careful not to add weeds as these will permeate the composted soil and cause damage when spread. Nettles, however, are the exception, as they not only speed up the composting process but they also provide a rich source of nitrogen.

There can be no other
occupation like gardening in
which, if you were to creep
up behind someone at their
work, you would find
them smiling.

Mirabel Osler

To forget how to dig the earth and tend the soil is to forget ourselves.

Mahatma Gandhi

Ash from a bonfire, once cooled, is a rich potash for fruit trees. Spread the ash around the base of fruit trees for a bumper harvest.

If you have a friend who keeps horses, offer to shovel some of the manure every once in a while. The manure is fantastic for your crops and your horsey friend will be grateful too!

The next time you have a cup of tea, don't throw the teabag away, instead, tear it open and sprinkle the dregs on the lawn as an instant fertiliser. Coffee grounds are equally beneficial.

Crystallised Epsom salts mixed with tepid water will pep up ailing tomato plants.

Rather than throwing old leather shoes away, bury them in the garden! They will slowly biodegrade, releasing enriching nutrients into the soil.

The unsightly algae that collects on the surface of ponds can be used as an effective alternative to shop-bought fertilisers.

If you have a private garden, urinating on your compost heap will pay dividends!

It's far cheaper to buy seeds than plants, so don't be tempted to buy young plants from the garden centre.

Avoid expensive mistakes when buying plants by resisting impulse buys and researching the type of plants that will thrive in the type of soil, terrain and aspect that your garden has.

Try discount retailers when buying plants, or buy out of season. Just a little bit of extra care, and the plants are just as healthy as the ones you'll find in the more upmarket nurseries.

Don't overbuy seeds – share the amounts
with a group of friends and then have a
seedling swap so you can exchange any
unwanted plants for ones that you do want.

Shop around for cheap seeds, such as in
end-of-season sales, and even on eBay.

Cuttings are one of the best ways to propagate new plants in your garden for free. If a neighbour or friend has a plant that you like the look of, take a cutting, but make sure you ask first!

Another way to obtain free seeds and seedlings is to join your local Freegle group where people can offload their excess seedlings and even unwanted garden equipment. Log on to ilovefreegle.org.

Use cellophane from packaged flowers to gather seeds from your favourite blooms. Tie the cellophane loosely around the plant to collect the seeds.

When storing leftover seeds, always use an airtight metal container. Make sure you label them to avoid adding bulbs to your dinner!

If there are aspects of gardening that you particularly dislike, try bartering your gardening time with friends and neighbours so that you can do jobs for each other.

Rather than forking out on a landscape gardener, apply some simple tricks to make your garden look more designed, such as shaping your lawn into a square or a circle, using a turf cutter for a professional-looking finish.

If you have a garden that doesn't receive a lot of sunlight, get a piece of hardboard or wood, cover it in foil and angle it towards the sun so that it reflects on the plants.

Waste water from washing up is perfect for watering gardens. Bath water can also be used to water the garden but it's best not to use it on edible crops.

Gardening requires lots of water – most of it in the form of perspiration.

Lou Erickson

Our England is a garden,
and such gardens
are not made
By singing: – 'Oh, how
beautiful!' and sitting in
the shade.

**Rudyard Kipling,
'The Glory of the Garden'**

THE HERB GARDEN

Cut lavenders at the end of summer, place in paper bags and dry slowly in an airing cupboard or boiler room. The lavender can be used to fill decorative bags that can be hung as air fresheners and moth repellents.

Cut fresh herbs, chop them and store in a bag in the freezer. This way you can have fresh herbs all year round.

Grow peppermint and make a wonderful
infusion by cutting the herb and placing the
leaves in a cup. Drench with boiling water
and steep for five minutes or so. Much nicer
than shop-bought teabags.

After a hard day in the garden, rub elder
leaves into your elbows to reduce stiffness
and aches.

In the same way that chamomile can soothe a person who is feeling out of sorts, it can also be used to give an ailing plant a lift when planted beside it.

Dandelions may be viewed as weeds in the grass, but they are high in vitamins and minerals and the young, tender leaves can be used in summer salads or blanched as a vegetable. Gather the leaves before the flowers form.

To dry herbs from the garden: Cut and remove any dry or diseased leaves. Shake gently to remove any insects or rinse with cool water and pat dry with paper towels. Remove the lower leaves along the bottom inch or so of the branch.

Bundle 4–6 branches together and tie as a bunch using string or a rubber band. The bundles will shrink as they dry and the rubber band will loosen, so check periodically that the bundle is not slipping. Make small bundles if drying herbs with high water content. Punch or cut several holes in a paper bag. Label the bag with the name of the herb to be dried and place the herb bundle upside down into the bag. Gather the ends of the bag around the bundle and tie closed. Hang the bag upside down in a warm, airy room and check in about two weeks to see how things are progressing. Keep checking weekly until the herbs are dry and ready to store.

The garden is the poor
man's apothecary.

German proverb

A garden is always a series
of losses set against a few
triumphs, like life itself.

May Sarton

Place dried lavender flowers in cotton teabags to create home-made lavender sachets. Place them in drawers to keep clothes smelling fresh.

Fill a muslin bag with 4 tablespoons of dried flowers and 1 tablespoon of unscented bath salts. Dangle the bag under the warm water as it runs from the tap, then place it directly in the water for a therapeutic bath. Remove the bag and let it dry between baths.

Store your dried herbs in airtight containers in a cool, dark place. They should remain fresh for up to two years.

Dill and coriander are best planted in a shady spot as they can quickly go to seed when placed in direct sunlight. Harvest the leaves regularly to encourage steady growth.

Basil grows best in a warm climate. Grow them either indoors or in a sheltered spot with the top half of a drinks bottle covering it to protect it from the elements.

A lemon balm plant is most useful to have in the garden. The aroma of lemon balm repels mosquitoes so as to provide a natural insect repellent. Pick a few fresh leaves, crush them in the hand to release the scent, and then rub them directly onto skin.

To help potted herbs grow better keep the soil fertilised with bananas which are a good source of potassium. Cut up pieces of banana peel and add directly to the soil. (They can also be added to soil around outdoor plants.)

Basil, oregano, chives, parsley and coriander are good garden companions to tomatoes because their aromatic foliage tends to repel insects that attack the fruit and leaves. Although there is no documented proof, many gardeners swear that growing basil next to tomatoes improves the taste of the tomatoes.

Give your mint an extra strong flavour by planting chamomile next to it.

Make your own mint sauce rather than paying for it. Pick two large handfuls of the freshest leaves, wash and chop them into tiny pieces and place in a serving bowl. Add four tablespoons of white wine vinegar, four tablespoons of hot water and one tablespoon of caster sugar. Allow to cool and serve.

Keep an aloe vera plant on your windowsill.
The sap in the leaves can be applied to
soothe scalds and dry skin.

Herbs have wonderful healing properties.
Here are a few simple herbal remedies for
tired gardeners to try:

If you've been on your feet all day, make up a basin or bucket of warm water, add in some lavender, sage or mint leaves and let your feet revive in the water.

If you've got a cold coming on, try inhaling an infusion of fresh rosemary or dried hollyhock flowers in boiling water, or drink tea containing fresh lemon balm leaves.

If your back is hurting after all that digging, gather a selection of strong-scented herbs, such as lavender and rosemary, and add these to oil; this can be sesame, almond, olive, or vegetable oil. Heat the oil and herbs on a low heat for five minutes, then leave to cool and add a few drops of essential oil if desired. Strain and decant the infusion into a dark-coloured glass bottle and get someone to rub the aches away.

Scattering fresh herbs onto charcoal at a barbecue will create a wonderful aroma while waiting for the food to cook.

Parsley can take a while to germinate, so it's one of the few plants that are best bought from a garden centre. Snip off the leaves regularly with scissors, but be careful not to trim it too much as excess cutting can destroy the plant.

HOUSE PLANTS

Use a windowsill to create a miniature salad garden, or fill a light area with potted flowers and fruit.

To provide a bit more light for house plants, place a piece of foil onto the wall next to the plant to reflect more light onto it.

Mint plants placed on the windowsill in
summer will keep flies and mosquitoes
at bay.

A fresh bundle of nettles at an open window
or door will also repel wasps and flies.

Don't buy flowers from the florist at the start of the week because they are likely to have been there since the weekend and won't last as long.

When making a flower arrangement, always trim off the leaves that will fall below the water level in the vase. Keeping the leaves on will make the water turn green and smell bad.

Support the heavy heads of cut tulips by sticking a pin just below the head on each stem. A few one pence and two pence pieces in the vase water will have the same effect.

Keep cut flowers fresh by adding a few drops of bleach to the water in the vase.

Add a small amount of salt to a vase of tulips
as this slows the opening of the
flower heads.

Crush the ends of rose stems to allow them
to take in more water; this will prolong
the display.

I don't know whether nice
people tend to grow roses or
growing roses makes
people nice.

Roland A. Browne

I've had enough of
gardening – I'm just about
ready to throw in the trowel.

Anonymous

Cut poppies will last longer if you singe the
bottoms of their stems.

Lilies contain vibrant orange pollen which
can stain fabric and carpets. Before making
your arrangement, trim the pollen off
with scissors.

Just as foxgloves are very beneficial
to other plants when planted in the
garden, they maintain their medicinal
values when cut, and when placed in an
arrangement they will prolong the life of
their fellow plants.

Try arranging flowers with short stems in a
bowl of wet sand as this will make them last
twice as long as those placed in water.

If you want a particularly special bloom to be preserved for years, place the flower in a screw-top jam jar with some surgical spirit. Leave for a few days to allow the flower to absorb some of the spirit and then top up the jar to the brim with surgical spirit and screw the lid on tightly.

Keep pot plants away from windowsills at night in winter – the cold could kill off the plants.

African violets make colourful and hardy houseplants. Use the leftover water from boiling eggs (when cooled) to water them as they will thrive from the calcium boost. Never water them from the tops as this can make their stems rot – place the plant on a saucer and water at the base.

Houseplants love to drink your leftovers, whether it's cold tea, wine or beer! As with people, they will need a touch of water to wash it down.

Make plant food for your house plants by
grinding up egg shells and mixing this with
the same amount of caster sugar.

Encourage children to get into gardening by
helping them to plant some quick-growing
seeds such as cress, mustard
and sunflowers.

BUDGET
BLOOMS

When considering what to grow, think about plants that are a good long-term investment and will provide interest throughout the year as well as year-on-year. Evergreens will provide flowers, berries and year-round foliage, and hardy perennials will bloom every year as opposed to annuals which you will need to re-sow each year.

See if your friends or neighbours will club together to bulk-buy bulbs directly from nurseries as this will be much cheaper than buying small amounts for yourself.

Protect newly planted bulbs from squirrels
and other small creatures by adding a layer
of chicken wire to the surface of the
planted area.

Dig up non-hardy bulbs as soon as they
have finished flowering to protect them from
frost damage. Store them in a pair of old
tights or stockings, tying a knot between
each bulb as this will prevent the spread
of disease.

Many garden centres have a bargain basement section – these are project plants and will require nurturing to bring back to health but the sense of satisfaction to be had when they thrive is enormous.

As with vegetables, aim to buy seeds rather than young plants – you pay a premium for petals.

Compared to gardeners, I
think it is generally agreed
that others understand very
little about anything
of consequence.

Henry Mitchell

What is a weed? A plant
whose virtues have not yet
been discovered.

Ralph Waldo Emerson

Old banana skins are rich in potassium and will do wonders for rose bushes when buried deep into the soil beside them.

Sunflowers will thrive around your compost heap, and when they grow tall they will screen the heap from the rest of the garden.

Encourage fuchsias to grow by laying chopped green bracken under the roots when you plant them. Green bracken is also good for covering the plants in cold weather.

Foxgloves have medicinal purposes and keep disease at bay when planted near your crops and blooms.

Flowers can be used for all manner of culinary delights. Here are some ideas for inspiration in the kitchen:

• Courgette flowers can be deep-fried in batter or stuffed with cheese and herbs and gently fried for an accompaniment to pasta.

- Nasturtium and pansy flower heads make a peppery addition to a salad, as well as adding a pretty splash of colour to green leaves.

- Violets make beautiful cake decorations when dipped in egg white and dusted with icing sugar.

• Elderflowers can be made into cordial and the heads are delicious when fried in a basic batter mix.

• Marigolds are easy to grow and can be used as an alternative to expensive saffron – they have a light and delicate flavour and their petals can be used to colour food.

CONTAINER GARDENS

Make spring planters. In a good-sized pot, plant layers of bulbs, starting with daffs/tulips/crocuses – the blooms will appear in early spring and as each variety comes to its end, the next variety will come to life giving you a beautiful showpiece right into early summer.

Make a hanging basket liner by cutting up an old jumper. They hold the compost very well and you can cut holes into them for planting.

Watering hanging baskets can be messy, with torrents of muddy water pouring from underneath them. To prevent this happening and to keep your plants well watered, place ice cubes on top of the soil.

Recycle polystyrene packaging by breaking it up and placing it in the bottom of garden tubs. This reduces the amount of compost that you will need and it makes the tubs much lighter and transportable.

Keep your used teabags and dry them. They are great for covering holes in large containers and prevent compost from being swept away when you water the plants.

If you are potting on, a clever tip is to put the smaller pot inside the bigger one and fill around it with soil so that the space left when you lift the small pot out is the right size for the plant.

A garden is not made in
a year; indeed it is never
made in the sense of finality.
It grows, and with the
labour of love should go
on growing.

Frederic Eden

Life begins the day you start a garden.

Chinese proverb

Window boxes can make the area around
them, including the windows, a little muddy.
To reduce this, pour gravel around
the plants.

Figs thrive when their roots are restricted,
making ideal container plants.

Get creative with planters for patios. All manner of things can be adapted, such as old chimney pots, tyres, wellington boots and old watering cans.

Dwarf fruit trees make ideal container plants. Choose from dwarf varieties of citrus trees and orchard fruits. Container trees don't reach the height of those planted in the ground but the fruit they produce will be of normal size and just as delicious.

Quince makes for a lovely patio plant,
providing both flowers and fruit.

Use up leftover pieces of charcoal after the
barbecue season is over by mixing them
with soil when potting plants, as this will
ventilate the soil and stop it from
becoming waterlogged.

WEEDS

In warm, dry weather leave small uprooted weeds on top of the soil where they will quickly dry out. In wet weather do not leave uprooted weeds on top as they will re-root. Gather them up and bury in the compost heap where they will quickly rot down.

Pick the tops off young nettles and cook for a very tasty vegetable dish, not dissimilar to spinach.

Broadleaf weeds are easy to identify by their broad, green leaves. Dandelions, clovers and plantains are among the most common and readily identifiable broadleaf weeds in lawns. Broadleaf weeds typically spread by seed and form isolated clumps that must be physically pulled from the base to ensure complete removal.

Always do your weeding in dry conditions and before the weeds have had the chance to come into flower. If you do your weeding in damp conditions, you will end up dividing and spreading the weeds over a larger area.

To remove the unsightly growth of weeds and grass between paving slabs, mix salt with boiling water and pour it over the cracks.

Stinging nettles contain essential vitamins A, C and D, and are high in minerals such as iron, potassium and calcium. They therefore make a useful tea. Pour near-boiling water over the herb and let steep for 5–10 minutes. Standard quantities are 75 g fresh or 30 g dried herb to 500 ml water. The infusion must be taken the same day. It may be sweetened, but do not add milk. (Warning: Use gloves to handle the leaves.)

If you water it and it dies, it's a plant. If you pull it out and it grows back, it's a weed.

Gallagher

One year's seeding makes
seven years' weeding.

English proverb

Perennial weeds such as couch grass, horsetail and bindweed quickly develop underground networks of roots. Remove them carefully by hand as the smallest piece of root left in the soil will quickly throw up new shoots. Dig out all fragments using a fork, then burn or dispose of them at the rubbish tip.

Weeds that have long taproots such as dandelions can survive without soil or water for many months. It is unlikely the compost heap will heat up enough to destroy them so it is safer to put them in the dustbin.

To clear previously uncultivated land of perennial weeds cut down any tall specimens, then cover the area with old carpet, thick cardboard or heavy-duty black polythene. Weigh the covering down with bricks to prevent it being blown off. Total exclusion of light will kill most weeds within a season. The more persistent varieties such as dandelions can take up to a year to die out completely.

After collecting up unwanted moss, leave it to darken and die, then spread it onto the garden as an acidifying mulch. Azaleas, camellias, heathers and heaths in particular will benefit.

Moss makes a useful cushion for pot plants.
When it is placed as a lining between the
holder and the pot, its moisture-retentive
qualities create a humid atmosphere and
stop the pot drying out. Moss also helps to
insulate the plant roots from extremes of
heat and cold.

Remove weeds without weedkiller, as this
can be harmful to pets, by digging the
offenders out with a knife or narrow-bladed
trowel. Try to dig out the roots to prevent
regrowth without disturbing the lawn
too much.

Plant a twig into the ground next to bindweed. The bindweed will curl round the twig, making it easier to target the weed and pull it out.

Burdock roots, once cleaned and chopped, can be a tasty addition to stir-fries.

Although it's classed as a weed, clover is very good for lawns as it boosts the nitrogen in the soil and it can be mown. It also attracts bees and prevents less attractive and more harmful weeds from taking up the space.

Yarrow is an unpopular weed but don't be too hasty to remove it, as it improves the quality of the soil and repels pests.

CHEAP AND FRIENDLY PEST AND DISEASE CONTROL

Butterflies are repelled by the smell of tomato plants, so plant these amongst your leeks to prevent them from laying eggs on your crop.

Instead of buying copper bands to go round pots to keep the slugs off, apply Vaseline around the rims of the pots – it's just as effective and much cheaper.

Twist a thin strip of tinfoil around the base of your cabbage plants to stop the cabbage fly from nibbling at them.

Outsmart the white cabbage moth by laying a few pieces of scrunched up kitchen towel around cabbages and broccoli. This will lead the moth to believe that the territory is already patrolled by other moths and they won't lay eggs there.

A past-repair garden hose can be cut into pieces to resemble snakes. Paint stripes on them and distribute round the garden to deter rodents and birds.

Curls of lemon and orange peel will have a similar effect – even cats will keep away.

A garden is a grand teacher.
It teaches patience and
careful watchfulness; it
teaches industry and thrift;
above all it teaches
entire trust.

Gertrude Jekyll

No two gardens are the same. No two days are the same in one garden.

Hugh Johnson

Deal with pest problems organically. For instance, you can entice slugs away from tempting plants by positioning beer wells nearby – slugs will be lured towards the pungent smell and away from your plants. Or crush eggshells and sprinkle around the base of tender plants to avert the destructive munching of slugs and snails.

To eradicate mildew on your cabbages, spray them with water mixed with methylated spirits.

Clubroot is particularly common in cabbages. Reduce the risk of this disease by burying sticks of rhubarb alongside the young cabbages as you bed them in.

Retain small yogurt pots and washing balls and balance these upside down on canes planted in the garden. The rattling noise will scare the birds away. They also save you from impaling yourself on sharp ends!

Vaseline applied to the trunks of fruit trees
will make it impossible for slugs to slime
their way to your harvest.

To trap earwigs in the garden, sink an oily
tuna can into the earth to ground level where
the earwigs seem numerous and fill it with
equal parts of used vegetable oil and soy
sauce. Instead of soy sauce you could use
an apple slice. Empty the can each morning.

Nasturtiums will repel a wide range of harmful insects and make an excellent companion plant. When planted in between rows of vegetables like cabbages, broccoli and broad beans they will keep pests such as blackfly away. They can also be planted under fruit trees as a trap for pests.

Season your garden with black pepper to discourage cats from using it as an outside toilet.

Molehills are very unsightly. A humane method of sending moles packing is to plant glass bottles (without lids on) into the molehills with the top of the bottle showing, so that the noise of the wind travels through their tunnels, encouraging them to move to a more peaceful location.

Make bird-scarers by upending brightly coloured plastic drinks bottles on garden canes and planting them in the soil amongst your crops.

If grasshoppers appear to be nibbling their way through your garden, plant coriander around the perimeter – the little creatures hate the smell.

Spray aphids with a bottle of soapy water.

Keep birds away from your grass seed and precious plants by making a garland of shiny objects. Thread foil, CDs, old cutlery and bottle tops onto garden string and hang from trees and hedges so that they flap in the wind.

GARDEN CREATURES

Consider purchasing a couple of hens. Rescue battery hens can cost from as little as fifty pence each. Once they are settled, they can lay up to five eggs a day as well as patrolling the garden for pests and plucking out weeds.

Leave some broken terracotta pots and rotting logs in dark corners in the garden as they make great homes for frogs and toads, and other beneficial insects.

Encourage slow-worms, ladybirds and bumblebees into the garden as they will hoover up the aphids, slugs and snails. The best way to tempt these useful creatures into the garden is to have an area of wild garden with long grass, piles of stones and wood and fallen leaves, as this will provide the ideal habitat for them to thrive.

Numbers of bees have dwindled in recent years but you can do your bit by planting a bee-friendly garden, with crocuses, snowdrops and heathers in spring; buddleia, thyme and lavender in the summer; and flowering privet and ivy in the winter.

Don't wear perfume in the garden – unless you want to be pollinated by bees.

Anne Raver

How fair is a garden amid
the trials and passions
of existence.

Benjamin Disraeli

Leave out your leftover carrots and apples for the squirrels.

Ladybirds consume around a hundred aphids a day. Attract these useful insects by hanging bundles of cow parsley in sheltered spots around the garden.

Hedgehogs are brilliant at devouring slugs.
Encourage these prickly creatures into the
garden by putting out a mixture of moist and
dry dog food. Never give them bread and
milk as this upsets their digestive system
and can make them very ill.

Pet rabbits are great for weeding and
trimming the lawn in the spring. Make sure
they have a lightweight run which can be
moved around the lawn. Their used bedding
can also be composted.

Primroses not only herald the start of spring,
but they also attract finches into the garden.

Put up nest boxes – simple DIY ones can be
made by following instructions available on
the Internet. Make the boxes and entry holes
different sizes to encourage tits, robins and
even owls to nest there.

Make fat balls for the birds in winter by melting lard and mixing in nuts, seeds, raisins, bacon rind and breadcrumbs. Collect some yogurt pots, carefully make a hole in the bottom of each one and thread a length of string through each and tie a knot at the bottom. Fill the cartons with the lard mixture and place in the fridge to harden. Once the mixture has set, cut away the yogurt pots and hang the fat balls on branches and fences, but be sure that they are out of reach of predators.

If you want to be happy
for a short time, get drunk;
happy for a long time, fall in
love; happy for ever, take
up gardening.

Arthur Smith

Who has learned to garden
who did not at the same
time learn to be patient?

H. L. V. Fletcher

WILD FORAGING

Wild food foraging is becoming increasingly popular, and it has many benefits, including: it is pesticide-free, it can be picked close to home, and it means making the most of seasonal produce that grows in the local countryside. It is essential to respect the law when gathering or collecting, so inform yourself of rare species and harvest sustainably. Wherever picking, do not take too much at the same time.

Food Safety: Do not gather from the sides of busy roads as the plants will be polluted. Do not pick from low down near pathways where dogs may have been.

Fungi and mushrooms

There are about 17 known deadly poisonous fungi and 65 poisonous fungi. Do not consume anything unless you are certain it's edible and then only consume small amounts on the first occasion to make sure your digestive system allows it. Gather with an experienced picker and buy yourself a good mushroom guide.

The chanterelle mushroom is an edible fungi, with a distinctive yellow flesh and a tunnel-shaped cap. Its forking gills run all the way down the stalk and it has a distinctive sweet scent. The chanterelle mushroom forms symbiotic associations with hardwoods and conifer trees, so it tends to grow in the same area each year. It has a peppery flavour and is a good source of vitamins A and D.

The giant puffball grows in meadows and on the edges of woodland, appearing suddenly. It is available to pick between July and November. It is almost the size of a football – a white globe with fungal fibres that connect it to the ground. The flesh must be white when cut into – if yellowing or grey then it's no longer edible. It can be cut into pieces and fried.

The cep mushroom is also known as porcini and has a large brown cap that looks like a bun. It grows singly or in clusters around woodland clearings and is ready for picking between August and November. It can be fried simply with butter and seasoning.

Seaweed

There are over 650 different varieties of seaweed to be found around the British coast, some of which are edible. The most common and easily identified seaweeds include carragheen, dulse, laver, tangle/oarweed, wracks and sea lettuce.

Seaweeds are packed with nutrients as they absorb and concentrate them directly from the surrounding water. Yet this ability to absorb nutrients also means that they absorb pollutants.

It is recommended that living seaweeds attached to rocks should be collected, and not harvested from the strand line. Always wash first before eating. Cooking methods will vary according to the individual seaweed.

Dulse *(Palmaria palmata)* is delicious eaten raw, sun-dried first. It can be added to stir-fries and soups, and is traditionally mixed with mashed potato in Ireland. Its dark red to brown fronds are long with divided tips. Dulse is best collected from May to September, found among the shoreline's rocks.

Plants

Common sorrel has a slightly sour taste and can be eaten in salads, added to sandwiches or cooked like spinach. It has an oval-shaped green leaf which has two lobes at the base, pointing downwards. It grows on grassy banks and low down on hillsides.

Wild garlic is found in ancient woodland. It has clusters of white starry flowers and long, spear-shaped leaves and has a strong garlicky aroma. The leaves and flowers can be chopped up and added to salads, soup or sauces.

Nettles are commonplace in moist woodlands and along rivers. Harvest them to make a beverage, but only use the younger, smaller plants and wear gardening gloves. Wash, then boil until the water goes green. Remove the leaves and add some lemon or sugar for flavour.

Sphagnum moss is soft to the touch, and can be recognised by its tiny green leaves which are toothed and grow in tufts close to the stem. It has antiseptic properties so can be used to clean a wound by rubbing the leaves over the skin. It can also be used to clean bowls and cups if no washing-up liquid is available. It is found on boggy ground in large patches.

Horseradish is a plant found growing on wasteland all around Britain. It can often be mistaken for dock leaves, but when horseradish leaves are crushed they give up their distinctive smell. The taproot extends deeply into the soil, but, as with any other plant, it is illegal to uproot horseradish without the landowner's permission. This taproot is what is made into a sauce with its hot, sharp flavour and can be dug up at any time of year. The young leaves can also be added to salads.

Fruit

Blackberries are probably the most well-known wild fruit that many of us have gathered from hedgerows and patches of waste ground. They are ready to pick between July and October and they freeze well.

Sloes are blue-black fruits that grow on blackthorn hedgerows throughout the country. They are ready to pick after the first frost in autumn. Wear gloves to avoid the sharp thorns. Their strong flavour makes them ideal for sloe jelly, delicious with meat and sausages, and can also be made into sloe gin.

In an orchard there should
be enough to eat, enough to
lay up, enough to be stolen
and enough to rot on
the ground.

James Boswell,
The Life of Samuel Johnson

Taste every fruit of every
tree in the garden at
least once.

Stephen Fry

Rose hips are a rich source of vitamin C.
They grow on the dog rose shrub which
flowers between May and July, followed by
bright red-orange hips in August. Both the
hips and the petals can be made into tea
and the hips make a rich, sweet syrup.
Dog rose hedgerows are common
around the countryside.

Wild strawberries are smaller than the
commercial strawberry. The fruit ripens in
late spring and early summer, often hiding
beneath the veined leaves. They can be
found in woodland and grassland. Add to
fruit salads, pancakes and other desserts.

The elderberry can often be found alongside blackberries. They should not be eaten raw but can be made into a rich syrup packed with vitamins A and C, or added to apples to make jam. Both the elderberries and elderflowers can be made into wine. The creamy white flowers bloom in late spring and early summer, followed by the bunches of red berries which ripen to purple-black from late August until November.

Herbs

Lemon balm is a citrusy herb that has been used in cooking and medicine for centuries. It can be used in recipes to replace lemon rind and can be made into tea to ease headaches and aid digestion. It has veined light green leaves and yellow flowers. The best time to pick lemon balm leaves is in April and May. It can be an invasive plant and is found across wasteland, preferring part-shade.

Fennel has become naturalised across limestone and chalky soils. It is often found near the sea. All parts of this herb are edible including the small bulb and the leaves. These can be chopped and added to salads, potatoes or fish dishes. It also makes a refreshing tea. The leaves can be picked for eating in late winter or early spring.

Water mint is a herb with red stems and oval, toothed leaves which are best picked between April and October. They can be used like garden mint to make tea or added to sauces for flavouring. The plant grows in damp places such as riverbanks, beside lakes and on marshland.

Nuts

Beechmast nuts can be collected beneath beech trees and eaten raw. They are brown kernels with arrow-shaped shells which need to be peeled off before eating the flesh inside.

Hazelnuts or cobnuts are ready to gather from August onwards. They are found in woods and hedgerows where the small trees grow. The nuts are rich in B vitamins and several other nutrients, making just a handful eaten a day a great protection against many common heart diseases.

Sweet chestnuts are ripe when the fruit has fallen in their prickly shells, around October and November. They are found beneath chestnut trees in parks and woodland all over Britain. The nuts can be roasted by taking off their green cases, making a slit in the shell, then placing them into an open fireplace. Chestnuts are also made into puree which can be used in casseroles and stuffing.

MAKE DO AND MEND

£4.99

ISBN: 978 1 84953 285 3

'A stitch in time saves nine.'

Proverb

THRIFTY ADVICE FOR HOMEMAKERS

Don't let being cash-strapped hold you back from having a house and garden to be proud of! This little book offers sage advice on how to use your precious resources of time, energy and money effectively to make a cosy, happy home. With tips on mending, upcycling, cleaning and gardening interspersed with witty quotations, this is an essential addition to every household.

BAKE FOR BRITAIN

£4.99

ISBN: 978 1 84953 267 9

'Come along inside... We'll see if tea and buns can make the world a better place.'

Kenneth Grahame

TASTY ADVICE FOR BRITISH BAKERS

Sumptuous scones with jam and clotted cream, lemon drizzle cake, Victoria sponge and brandy snaps – just a few of the sweet treats that get British taste buds tingling. So put on your apron, dig out the mixing bowl and start the oven because it's time to go baking mad.

Here's a book packed with recipes and quotations to help you bake your country proud.

If you're interested in finding out
more about our gift books follow us
on Twitter: @Summersdale

www.summersdale.com

DIG
FOR
VICTORY

DIG
FOR
VICTORY

DIG
FOR
VICTORY

DIG
FOR
VICTORY

DIG
FOR
VICTORY

DIG FOR VICTORY

DIG FOR VICTORY DIG FOR VICTORY

DIG FOR VICTORY DIG FOR VICTORY DIG FOR VICTORY

DIG FOR VICTORY DIG FOR VICTORY DIG FOR VICTORY

DIG FOR VICTORY DIG FOR VICTORY DIG FOR VICTORY

DIG FOR VICTORY DIG FOR VICTORY DIG FOR VICTORY